A big black bag was on the path next to the bin.

It was very smelly.

The cats kept away from it.

A rat crept up to the big black bag. He liked the smell of it. He bit the big black bag.

A banana skin and an egg-shell fell out of the big black bag. The rat did not like them.

He bit the big black bag again.

A crust of pizza and some crisps fell out of the big black bag.

Crunch, crunch went the rat on the crust of pizza.

Crunch, crunch went the rat on the crisps.

Then some fish and chips fell out of the black bag.

They were soft and very smelly.

Munch, munch went the rat on the very soft smelly fish and chips. Munch, munch. This was a very good lunch.

The very good lunch had gone.

The rat was very full.

He went back to his den and he went to sleep. Zzzzzz ... zzzzzz.